Copyright © 2023
Story, Job Descriptions & Activities courtesy of Marcia Rowe & Kelita Wood
of KidsTime2Play
www.kidstime2play.co.uk

Illustrations & Graphic Design by Cristina Pereyra & Claire Matches
www.squigglesforkids.com

Printed in the United Kingdom

BLISSETTS

First Printing, 2023
ISBN 978-1-7393171-0-2

Published by KidsTime2Play London

Introduction

This is the second book in our collection of Time2Play stories. In our first book, Marc learns about patience and important skills children need socially. He attends a children's activity class and has lots of fun making new friends.

Our stories support children around the Early Years Foundation Stages (EYFS) in a range of settings. Each story has a theme based on early life experiences that help shape healthy social interactions. The fun begins with joint reading, followed by an educational discussion before the activities at the back of the book.

What is Time2Play?

Time2Play helps children to learn, laugh and play as they gain new skills and build positive friendships. Educational activities and games are themed to promote positive life values and life skills for child development. We encourage teamwork for group learning and self-discovery.

The teacher or play practitioner encourages inclusivity. Everyone is empowered to feel motivated to participate in the play activities and educational workshops. At the end of a Time2Play class, we celebrate the children's achievements.

Time2Play aims to:

Promote reading from an early age with our collection of books

Encourages self-expression and creative writing for future success

Encourages conversations to build social confidence

Encourages positive and healthy experiences with each other

Time2Play

CAREERS WEEK WITH MARC AND FRIENDS

This book is inspired by Marc and friends, who are confident young learners.

The morning finally arrived.

Marc's day was about to change at the Time2Play class.

He looked forward to going every week, but today was different.

He had a very important job to do!

Marc wanted moral support from his two besties, Keion and Kavell, and had invited them to come along.

During the last class, his teacher had asked for him to be their special penguin mascot.

"Oh Wow! Can I do this?"

"Oh Wow! this is going to be epic"

Marc thought.

Once Marc got washed and dressed, he <u>nervously</u> looked down at the list he was given with his tasks.

The words <u>appeared</u> to be jumping out at him as he stared in <u>amazement</u> at what he was going to do.

As Marc was <u>reading</u> his tasks, he <u>paused</u>, looked up and spotted himself in the mirror.

Looking startled, Marc moved closer to the mirror.

He bumped his beak, "What! My beak is so big, man!"

In his mind, he can hear the reassuring words from his mum reminding him that he will be ok.

Soon afterwards, Marc and his mum left to go to the Time2Play class.

Time2Play Penguin Mascot Job Description

1. To have fun with children and families.

2. To have a good sense of humour.

3. To be kind and friendly to others.

4. To enjoy music and dancing.

5. To be organised.

Look at my duties above! Mascots dress up in their outfit to entertain children and families.

Upon arrival, Marc felt very nervous. Marc had a feeling like he had <u>butterflies</u> inside his tummy.

Everyone looked <u>surprised</u>!

They did not know a Mascot was coming today.

Marc <u>realised</u> how <u>different</u> he looked.

The teacher reached for his hand and asked,

"What is your name?"

Marc took a deep breath and proudly announced,

"My name is Dancy the penguin!"

With laughter in their voices, Keion and Kavell both pointed and said,

"Hold on a minute. That's Marc!".

Marc moved around to confirm that it was him.

Now he was ready to kick-start the musical games, which was a task on his list.

At the end of the class, Marc used that time to reflect with his mum and teacher.

They complimented him on his achievements.

He felt very proud.

Marc felt so happy he asked his teacher if everyone could dress up next time. The teacher suggested a careers week and said,

"This time, everyone can explain their chosen job role".

Marc smiled and agreed this was a fantastic idea.

He could not wait to share the news and to showcase his new Black Panther superhero outfit.

The following week, the children arrived. They looked GREAT!

The policewoman looked very professional. The fireman looked fearless as he stood close to the bold builder. The cheeky chef gazed at the dedicated doctor and the talented teacher noticed the footballer's fidgety feet.

Each child had a turn to talk about their job role and their special skills. Marc spoke about his job as a Time2Play mascot.

His confidence had grown!

Let's read all about our different jobs!

Police Officer
Job Description

1. To have good communication skills.

2. To be a law abiding person.

3. To be able to solve crimes.

4. To be physically fit.

5. To keep people safe.

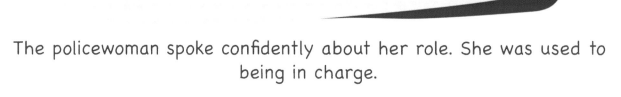

The policewoman spoke confidently about her role. She was used to being in charge.

Fireman
Job Description

1. To act quickly and safely under pressure.

2. To give and receive clear instructions.

3. To have first aid and rescue skills training.

4. To have good communication skills.

5. To be a team player.

The fireman spoke clearly with a big voice to explain his role. He was used to speaking loudly during emergencies.

Chef
Job Description

1. To have good communication skills.

2. To create delicious meals.

3. To be organised and focused.

4. To have an eye for details.

5. To work safe in the kitchen.

The chef spoke in a jolly voice. Her cheeks were flushed, as though she had just arrived from the kitchen.

Doctor
Job Description

1. To have good communication skills.

2. To give first aid and save lives.

3. To make dificult decisions.

4. To know about the human body.

5. To be caring and understanding.

The doctor was calm and confident, as he spoke about his role working for the NHS.

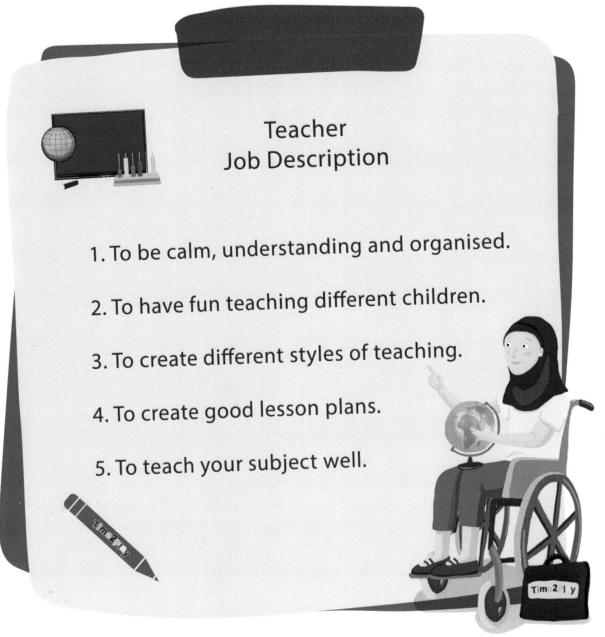

Teacher
Job Description

1. To be calm, understanding and organised.

2. To have fun teaching different children.

3. To create different styles of teaching.

4. To create good lesson plans.

5. To teach your subject well.

The teacher was excited to talk about her job. She spoke passionately about the importance of educating children.

Builder
Job Description

1. To have knowledge about construction.

2. To be good at planning with a team.

3. To understand health and safety.

4. To make good decisions.

5. To be good at planning tasks.

The builder looked strong and spoke very boldly about working as a team to build homes for families.

Footballer
Job Description

1. To have good communication skills.

2. To have good ball control.

3. To have good co-ordination.

4. To be physically fit and healthy.

5. To be a good team player.

The footballer wanted to show children his upper-kick skills. It is a great opportunity for children to learn in a practical way.

Black Panther
Job Description

1. To be responsible for keeping others safe.

2. To have good problem solving skills.

3. To show good leadership skills.

4. To be physically fit and healthy.

5. To make difficult decisions.

Black Panther is a symbol of strength and a protector of his country. He shows great leadership skills and always tries his best to overcome challenges.

Everyone had a turn to share and had a great time in the class.

Marc and Keion delightedly joined in a positive 'fist bump'.
It was a mark of respect for a job well done.

Kavell smiled and Keion said,
"We can achieve anything when we try our best!"

Exercise Your Mind and Activities

Now that you have read the story, please complete the activities.
Children can choose how they share their answers.

Activity Tools

You will need a writing pencil, coloured pencils and something to write on.

Getting Support

Choose an adult to help you with the activities.

Activity Instruction

Adults will support children's learning style and level of understanding in each activity.

Children will develop at their own pace and allow for equal turn taking in a group.

Activity One: Wordsearch

Activity Two: Multiple Choice Questions

Activity Three: Challenge Words

Affirmations 4 Kids

It's all about Kidstime2play

Activity One Wordsearch

Write the words below to help your search.

Ages under 5

Gra_s_s ✓

Br_i_c_k_s ✓

Dr_u_m ✓

B_o_y

B_ _ _l

M_a_t

G	M	L	D	R	U	M	L
R	G	L	A	R	D	Z	B
A	T	M	J	K	G	Z	R
S	T	C	A	K	I	S	I
S	G	C	J	T	R	B	C
W	G	B	A	L	L	B	K
W	F	O	E	D	H	N	S
R	F	Y	Q	B	E	D	L

It's all about Kidstime2play

Activity One Wordsearch

Write the words below to help your search.
Can you find this missing fruit? G_ _ _ _ _

P _ _ _ _ _

P _ _ _ _ _ _ _

T _ _

T	J	K	G	R	A	P	E	S	K	H	V
E	G	Y	C	W	B	M	N	E	Y	T	L
P	A	R	A	C	H	U	T	E	G	S	C
E	A	Y	Z	W	D	N	O	G	S	D	V
N	S	C	Z	B	E	L	P	P	A	J	X
C	S	V	H	T	F	N	I	D	W	K	I
I	H	T	L	I	G	M	P	J	B	R	A
L	H	S	O	T	L	F	Q	K	O	R	S
T	A	Q	X	P	H	D	A	H	O	O	P
L	S	R	W	I	S	S	R	D	K	T	D
A	F	U	O	O	J	L	D	E	I	D	W
D	F	K	P	E	N	G	U	I	N	S	B

C _ _ _ _ _ _ _

A _ _ _ _ _

S _ _ _ _

P _ _ _ _ _ _ _ _

Activity Two: Multiple-Choice Questions

Circle the correct answer

Children under 5 years old

1. What was Marc dressed up as?

a) dog   b) cat   c) penguin   d) zebra

2. What colour was the penguin's beak?

a) pink   b) blue   c) white   d) yellow

3. What two feelings did Marc have in the story?

a) sad   b) angry   c) nervous   d) happy

4. Marc said his tummy felt like it had insects inside it. What insect was it?

a) butterflies   b) ants   c) beetles   d) grasshoppers

5. Which person in the story gives medicine?

a) doctor   b) footballer   c) fireman   d) builder

Activity Two: Multiple-Choice Questions

Circle the correct answer

Children over 5 years old

1. Marc was chosen to be a mascot. What two feelings did he feel about it?

a) proud   b) sad   c) silly   d) nervous

2. What do we mean by 'epic'?

a) It's not good!   b) It's scary!   c) It's boring!   d) It's fantastic!

3. What does a positive 'fist bump' mean?

a) let's battle   b) I can't shake hands   c) to show respect   d) to play a game

4. What is the skill all the professionals have in common?

a) rescuer   b) communication   c) score goals   d) cooking

5. Why did the teacher hold Marc's hand in the class?

a) to make him feel supported   b) to stop Marc from talking
c) she had cold hands   d) Marc had warm hands

Activity Three: 1 Minute Challenge

Children under 5 years old

Can you find the objects or the actions in 1 minute?
Tick the box when you have found each one.
Ask your grown-up to time you.

1.   **The penguin's list of tasks**   ☐

2.   **The teacher in the wheelchair**   ☐

3.   **A child pointing**   ☐

4.   **Butterflies**   ☐

5.   **Children dancing**   ☐

6.   **The teacher**   ☐

1 MIN

How many words did you find in 1 minute?

Activity Three: Challenge Words

Children over 5 years old

Talk with your grown-up about these words and share your thoughts about their meaning.

1. **Besties** ☐

2. **Moral support** ☐

3. **Nervous** ☐

4. **Fidgety** ☐

5. **Talented** ☐

6. **Job role** ☐

How many new words from this list did you learn?

Affirmations 4 Kids

Choose your affirmation to start your day:

Think about using these new affirmations with your friends and family.

I will work hard and try my best.

Hard work pays off.

I am a team player.

Try, try, and try again!

Today may be gloomy, but tomorrow is a new day!

I can make things happen when I believe in myself!

I am beautiful inside and out.

I will be kind to myself.

Affirmations 4 Kids

Choose your affirmation to start your day:

Think about using these new words with your friends and family.

I will breathe and take my time.

Change comes with hard work, and I will get there.

Life can be challenging but I will stay focused.

Love myself no matter what – I am important!

Great results come from challenges.

Be proud of my achievements.

I will teach others what I have been taught.

I can do it!

Time 2 Play : Careers Week with Marc and Friends

About the Authors

Marica Rowe has many roles in her life. She is a wife, mother to Marc in the Time 2 Play sories; as well as a Registered Accredited Therapist with the British Association for Counselling and Psychotherapy (BACP) since 2006. Marcia has over 25 years of counselling experience and has been running successful businesses since 2005. She first set up Time 2 Talk Counselling in 2005 before her launch of Facet Therapy Ltd. in 2014. The services offer a variety of theraputic ways to connect with children, young people and families using approved theories and models. Marcia holds an Affiliate Membership with some of the top international Private Medical Insurance (PMI) companies to provide counselling to their employees.

Kelita Wood is an Associate Member of the Chartered Institute of Personnel & Development (CIPD), has an MA in Human Resources (2010). She is a HR professional with over 12 year's experience in various sectors and passionate about how individuals learn and develop their employability skills.

Kelita has been involved in running children's activities for Virgin Active and Time2Play before becoming the Business Manager for Facet Therapy in November 2019. As a mum of two and founder of Kids Employability Skills, Kelita's mission is to empower her own children and other young people with life skills and life values. In doing so, they will become great citizens and employable adults achieving their future aspirations.

To find out more, email Kelita.kidsemployability@outlook.com
Insta & FB @kids.employability

Acknowledgements

We Would Like to Thank

All our family and friends, including the educational settings for sharing our diverse stories with the wonderful children.

Another big thank you to Squiggles, who have done an amazing job creating the colourful images and designing the books.

A special thank you to Facet Therapy for the inspiration and the concept of Time2Play. You can find out more about the fantastic work they do with children, young people and families below:

To find out more, go to: www.facettherapy.co.uk
OR email : facettherapy@gmail.com – Insta, FB, LinkedIn @facettherapy

Get involved with our children's workshops

and be part of a community of amazing little authors!

Learn more at www.kidstime2play.co.uk

Look out for our first series!

Time2Play: Marc's First Visit
Available to purchase from Kidstime2play
Waterstones & Amazon

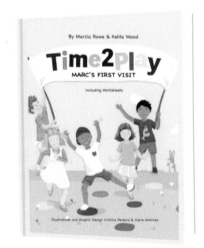

www.kidstime2play.co.uk
kidstime2play@hotmail.com

@kidstime2play  @kidst2p